T0384199

Bringing Mindfulness Into the Classroom

How can we help our students navigate challenges with confidence, mental well-being, and presence? While many schools implement social emotional learning or guidance programs, this book shows an easy, effective, and sustainable way to incorporate mindfulness into your classroom no matter what grade or subject you teach.

Tara Segree, recipient of the 2021 Innovative Educator Award and a collaborator of the Mini Meditations for Kids podcast, shows how mindful practices can help students build confidence, overcome anxiety, focus, engage in learning, find their strengths, and more.

Chapters provide tools and activities for incorporating mindfulness into your day-to-day teaching, as well as ideas for partnering with families so students can continue their practice at home. Special features include The 30-Day Mindfulness Challenge to give you an accessible way to try mindfulness with your students, and pages with journal prompts to help you on your own mindfulness journey.

Tara Segree is a Special Education English Teacher in Maryland and the co-creator of the Student Alliance for Flourishing. Tara was trained in mindfulness under the world-renowned expert and author davidji and Suze Yalof Schwartz of Unplug Meditation in Los Angeles, California.

Also Available from Routledge Eye
On Education
(www.routledge.com/K-12)

The Meditation and Mindfulness Edge: Becoming a Sharper, Healthier, and Happier Teacher
Lisa M. Klein

Mindfulness for Students: A Curriculum for Grades 3-8
Wendy Fuchs

Everyday Self-Care for Educators: Tools and Strategies for Well-Being
Carla Tantillo Philibert, Christopher Soto, and Lara Veon

Embracing Adult SEL: An Educator's Guide to Personal Social Emotional Learning Success
Wendy Turner

Bringing Mindfulness Into the Classroom

Easy Ideas You Can Try Tomorrow

Tara Segree

Routledge
Taylor & Francis Group

NEW YORK AND LONDON

Designed cover image: Getty

First published 2025
by Routledge
605 Third Avenue, New York, NY 10158

and by Routledge
4 Park Square, Milton Park, Abingdon, Oxon, OX14 4RN

Routledge is an imprint of the Taylor & Francis Group, an informa business

Library of Congress Cataloging-in-Publication Data
Names: Segree, Tara, author.
Title: Bringing mindfulness into the classroom: easy ideas
you can try tomorrow / Tara Segree.
Description: New York, NY: Routledge, 2025. |
Includes bibliographical references.
Identifiers: LCCN 2024029437 (print) | LCCN 2024029438 (ebook) |
ISBN 9781032832586 (hardback) | ISBN 9781032822501 (paperback) |
ISBN 9781003511847 (ebook)
Subjects: LCSH: Affective education. | Social learning. | Mindfulness
(Psychology) | Education—Social aspects. | Emotional intelligence.
Classification: LCC LB1072 .S43 2025 (print) | LCC LB1072 (ebook) |
DDC 370.15/34—dc23/eng/20230713
LC record available at https://lccn.loc.gov/2024029437
LC ebook record available at https://lccn.loc.gov/2024029438

ISBN: 978-1-032-83258-6 (hbk)
ISBN: 978-1-032-82250-1 (pbk)
ISBN: 978-1-003-51184-7 (ebk)

DOI: 10.4324/9781003511847

Typeset in Palatino
by codeMantra

Contents

Preface with Thoughts on Artificial Intelligence

The intention of this book is to help all of us (teachers, parents, students, community leaders, etc.) bring mindfulness into the classroom. Mindfulness is a way of life that allows us to be conscious as we walk through our day, better able to make decisions, respond to the challenges we are faced with, and let a ripple effect of peace wave out around us to others. Mindfulness reminds us to stop, breathe, and assess. Students are better able to learn when they are able to take moments to just feel their breath and say positive affirmations. They gain more confidence, since learning to sit in your heart and listen to it allows us to trust ourselves. Students are also able to focus better since they are training their minds to see a thought through mindfulness but then bring their attention back to their breath or mantra, or the task at hand in the classroom.

The intention of this book is to make mindfulness a norm in every classroom; that we take moments daily to be mindful and foster a culture that is conscious of their actions and decisions, thus bringing peace into the classroom and contributing to the space that builds confidence, collaboration, and creativity in every student, making our world a more peaceful planet.

This book offers a way to develop equity in the classroom for mental well-being; a human right that all should have access to. Use this book as a toolkit and bring in just one suggestion a week, to help your students and yourself as an educator. Use this book for professional development opportunities to foster a school climate that is centered around the well-being of students' mental health. This book can also be used as a workshop guide for parents so that the school climate of peace can move out into the community.

When we teach our students to become mindful, we teach them how to tap into their flourishing. All people should live a life of flourishing. Flourishing is the ability to thrive in life, to find joy in the everyday, and to know you are living with purpose. When we understand what it is that brings us true joy, then we can turn to those things to better know ourselves and our strengths. When we know our strengths, we become more confident in ourselves and are then able to collaborate with others and create.

This is also a resource for parents. Whether you homeschool your children or not, this can help you to understand the importance of allowing your children to be who they are, help them cultivate a positive mindset through mindfulness, and set them up for a life full of success, whatever that means to them.

Children of any age can use these tools. I have used all of these techniques with children as young as two to those young at heart at 88.

This book is also very timely, as we try to navigate a world of artificial intelligence, determining what is real, and what is fake, on the computers in the palm of our hands. We are all using our phones to gain information on everything, and this useful tool can help make our lives easier. We all know though that this tool can also cause depression as people have FOMO (Fear Of Missing Out), as they observe others only posting their highlights.

This book brings us back to our heart. Mindfulness allows us to listen to what our heart has to say and to determine where we should be placing our energy, according to what is important to us. But for us to know those answers, we need to listen to our heart; to tune out the rest of the noise of the world around us, as well as the noise in the palm of our hand. When we do that, we can make decisions that are for us. We can create our world to be one of peace. Artificial intelligence cannot give us those answers; only our heart can.

In a world of ChatGPT and artificial intelligence, mindfulness is a way to come back to your heart to remember what is real in life.

Artificial intelligence cannot know what is in the heart. Only we know what is in our hearts and where we want to direct our energy. Only we know our feelings toward what we love, what brings us joy, and what brings us peace. ChatGPT does not. Being mindful is not regulated by artificial intelligence. Being mindful, learning to be mindful, is taking our power back. This is a superpower as we take back our power, being in control of ourselves and what we truly want. Mindfulness is we being us, not regulated by artificial intelligence. More than ever, we need to learn how to be mindful so that we know what is real; what is real for us, and what unique ways we tap into our peace and joy.

This book is written in a conversational format, as if I am sitting across from you enjoying a cup of coffee; for when we have heartfelt conversation, it stokes the fire of genius and the pondering of thoughts and concepts. Pour yourself a cup of coffee or tea, and let's begin…

Foreword by Sep Riahi

In today's rapidly changing world, equipping young people with the ability to understand both their external environments and internal emotions is critical. Mindfulness, with its focus on developing resilience and emotional intelligence, is an invaluable skill for today's youth.

I first encountered Tara's outstanding work in mindfulness during a Harvard Flourishing Project webinar. Her dedication to improving children's well-being through these practices aligned perfectly with our goals at Global Tinker, sparking a partnership that has positively impacted children at all stages of life, from the US to Ukraine and beyond.

Tara's book is an indispensable resource for educators and parents alike. It offers a compelling and practical blueprint for embedding mindfulness into educational and parenting practices, emphasizing its importance for the holistic development of children. This book goes beyond merely outlining techniques; it is a clarion call for making mindfulness a foundational element in the upbringing of children.

Within this book, Tara provides insightful strategies and tools essential for supporting children in their educational journeys and personal growth. Her thorough approach to implementing mindfulness ensures that children are equipped not only for academic success but also for managing their emotional well-being.

As you explore this book, I hope you are inspired to integrate these practices into your interactions with young learners. By adopting these methods in educational settings and homes, we can help foster a generation that is academically adept, emotionally intelligent, and prepared to navigate the complexities of modern life.

With great anticipation and hope,

Sep Riahi

Sep Riahi is the CEO of Global Tinker, a multi-award-winning educational media company that inspires children's real-world discovery and exploration through world-class storytelling and constructionist pedagogy. Notably Global Tinker's "Mini Meditations for Kids" – a collaboration with Tara Segree – was named a top children's podcast by Common Sense Media. With over 20 years in high-impact media, Sep previously held senior roles at Sesame Workshop before co-founding Global Tinker. He holds degrees from the University of Texas and the University of Pennsylvania.

1

Why Mindfulness Is Essential in Our Classrooms Today

As educators, we come into our classrooms daily as life coaches. We are no longer just teaching colors and shapes, conventions of writing, characterization, history lessons, the Pythagorean theorem, or chemical reactions. We are now very aware and ethically responsible for picking up on mental health red flags. And not just because we were told in professional development to do so, but because we are noticing our students' angst and the amount of stress they are under. We feel the need to reach out to those students and make sure they are ok. The plight of the modern-day student cannot be ignored.

Educators have willingly or unwillingly taken on this role as life coaches. Our students are faced with obstacles never faced before by a society and need to learn to navigate these challenges with confidence and a creative mindset. Students' mental well-being, or their flourishing, must be addressed in our classrooms so that students are able to better tap into their critical thinking skills. They spend more awake time with teachers than their families, and we have a duty to help foster their independence and self-confidence, and guide them to learn to think for themselves. Bringing mindfulness into the classroom allows students to learn to look within themselves for answers, values, and their own opinions. At any age, students can gain confidence

DOI: 10.4324/9781003511847-1

in who they are and what is important to them. Once students are confident in themselves, they can then collaborate with others and create.

Teachers understand the need to connect with students and help them along their journey of life, at least for this school year, before passing them on to the next teacher. It should be one of our goals as educators: to pass students on who feel a little more confident in who they are, a little more loved, a little more of a good citizen with a purpose, no matter what their age. We can contribute to making our world a better place by helping our students connect to their hearts through mindfulness.

Mindfulness is a great tool for all children, especially for those who have issues with focusing, and we seem to have more and more students each year who are naturally and environmentally distracted. Through mindfulness, students learn to see those extra thoughts, but then are able to bring their awareness back to the task at hand. The more they practice mindfulness, the more they are able to place their attention where they need to. Adults can benefit from this practice as well.

We should be asking ourselves this question and then asking our students: How can I make this world a better place? Your answer can lead to your own personal flourishing. We are all different and that is a beautiful thing. We must teach to a student's strength even if it is different from how we see the world and how we learn. They are on a journey just like us. We want it to be a journey of flourishing and evolution into a better version of ourselves each day, week, month, and year. As teachers, we must flourish first to be able to set an example for our students and community.

We need to incorporate gratitude into our daily practice as well as in our classrooms. Where can you find moments of gratitude? That cup of coffee or tea? The gorgeous color of the leaves? Beautiful sky? The smile on a child's face? Preschoolers can discuss this or draw pictures and older students can journal and share.

Flourishing and becoming mindful does not happen overnight, but it does happen pretty quickly. Once you start living the way you were intended to live, with a heart full of peace and love, your whole outlook changes. You start to notice the beauty in the everyday, and the beauty in everyone.

Shrink the amygdala with meditation instead of enlarging it with the snooze button. Clear space, make space, and save space for what is to come in divine time. Trust that the universe/nature/God/your higher self has your best interest at heart. Sometimes a door closes because you were meant for something greater. Life is for you, not against you; have faith and trust that all is well. This outlook on life will help you to flourish.

What does the amygdala have to do with mindfulness? The amygdala is the part of the brain that regulates our emotions and can become overwhelmed with stress and/or depression, or shrink with calm and peacefulness. When we meditate or take time to be mindful, we allow our amygdala to function with a clear outlook and are able to make conscious choices aligned with love instead of fear.

When students have the opportunity to look within to realize their strengths, this gives them the confidence to collaborate and create with others. It is available to all students, regardless of their socioeconomic status. Wellness is a human right. Accessing personal flourishing or personal Zen by tapping into your heart is something we all need to learn how to do and value. Students who are exposed to mindfulness learn key tools that enable them to learn to walk on a path of peace throughout life. They learn to collaborate with others to solve what they think is important to their own life, community, and potentially even on a global scale. Students have the ability to collaborate across nations, borders, and language barriers, to help bring peace to our world with what this future generation deems important.

There are no limits with our students for we are fostering personal flourishing, community flourishing, and the ripple effect is global flourishing. We are making this world a better place by helping one student at a time learn to be mindful and conscious of their decisions and how they contribute to their community and world.

These are our future leaders: our politicians, CEOs, parents, and entrepreneurs. Let us spend just a few minutes each day giving our students the opportunity to tap into their heart, to listen, and to walk a path of peace in life. The ripple effect will only help our planet and the people who live on it. Our students will learn to collaborate with others and create solutions to global issues and bring peace to our planet.

All students deserve to learn how to be mindful. They deserve to tap into their heart to find their purpose which then contributes to their confidence. All students deserve to connect with other students to work collectively toward a meaningful goal that is from their own creation. Teachers need to see the value in the uniqueness of individuals and celebrate our diversity and uniqueness for that is what makes our planet beautiful.

Students who can think for themselves and be confident in themselves generate new ideas.

When we are mindful, we develop empathy and are open minded. We learn the value of listening to others from other backgrounds.

Mental wellness can be attained by everyone if given the tools and time to tap into their heart. Let us bring these life-changing tools into our classroom and watch our students grow toward the light with an optimistic outlook on life.

Bringing mindfulness into the classroom fosters mental wellness which is a human right and a form of equity. All students deserve and must learn tools of how to be mindful so that they can tap into their own internal peace at any time, thus making our world a more peaceful planet.

As educators, we control the energy in the room with our presence and our conscious classroom management. Your students will start to match your energy. So when you have peace and are conscious of who you are, what you enjoy, and what fulfills your life, you share that peace with your students and your students' energy changes for the better as well.

The generation of today needs to have confidence in themselves and in their strengths so that they can collaborate with others and create. They have been faced with challenges but have risen to those challenges and have learned to adapt and learn in ways never even thought to be the norm. And they have succeeded. We need to tell them how proud we are of them and how we value them. More importantly, they need to value themselves. That is where integration of personal flourishing comes into the classroom. We help students to recognize their gifts, their interests, and what makes them tick. They then can spend more time doing the things that bring personal fulfillment and joy, thus enabling them to walk a path with purpose and a life of optimism.

As we are well aware, some of our students are struggling to have their basic needs met. Academics come second next to finding their next meal or wondering if the lights will be on when they return home. Mindfulness offers a safe space. Students have the ability to access their heart and find internal peace, even though the external world is unpredictable and full of challenges that are out of their control.

Try It! Resources You Can Use in Your Classroom

In the next chapters, you will find Try It sections with specific activities to do throughout the chapters of this book. Mindfulness is as simple as just becoming aware: aware of your surroundings, aware of your body, aware of your breath. When you are noticing this moment, and consciously feeling how your body breaths, that is being mindful. When you are noticing the moment and bring your attention to something such as leaves blowing in the wind, the sounds of birds singing, the smile of a child, that is mindfulness. We do not have to sit in a semi-lotus position with Zen music playing in the background to be mindful. We just need to consciously be aware of our surroundings and notice.

Anyone can easily be taught the art of being mindful. Being an educator for over 18 years, I have taught students as young as two how to rest in their stillness and be mindful. These life-long skills then help us as human beings to walk a more peaceful path and respond to daily challenges creatively, with intention and clarity. Once we develop this skill, we organically walk through life aligned with love and peace. Mindfulness not only makes the individual kinder but our world kinder as well due to the ripple effect of peaceful energy from one human being to another. Mindfulness also helps with clarity, tapping into intelligence and newly learned information, the lessening of anxiety, optimum brain performance, and self-confidence.

Mindfulness can take place anywhere: the car, office chair, while waiting in line, taking a walk, in your home, etc.

2

How Can Mindfulness Help Teachers?

To bring mindfulness into our classrooms, we need to make sure that WE are doing okay. We need to have stability and balance in our own life. We need to make sure that we are flourishing. We want to bring flourishing into our classroom and teach children to tap into their own personal flourishing, but we cannot do that unless we ourselves are flourishing. We cannot pour from an empty cup. So we need to ask ourselves: Am I flourishing? Do I feel fulfilled in life? Do I have purpose in my life? Am I filled with joy on a daily basis? Do I laugh? Do I smile? Do I see the beauty in every day? Am I happy? I hope your answer is yes, but a lot of people answer no to the bulk of these questions, and maybe you do too. Before we can teach our students how to flourish, we must be flourishing ourselves.

So how do we flourish? By tapping into what makes you feel and embrace life. Is it exercise? Is it taking a walk in nature? Is it painting? Is it gardening? Playing an instrument? Is it journaling? Is it listening to some really great music? Is it dancing? Is it meditating? Is it photography? What is it? What is it that brings you joy? What is it that gets you out of bed in the morning? Whatever it is, do more of that!

We need to set up a routine of healthy habits to be the foundation of our day that then turns into our week, our month, year, and our life. We need to start each day having peace in our heart;

DOI: 10.4324/9781003511847-2

not springing up with the alarm, pressing snooze, and trying to drip every last second out of our sleep. According to a study published in the *Journal of Physiological Anthropology* in 2022, that is, actually, terrible for your mind as that snooze button never allows you to go back to full rest and only leads to grogginess for the rest of the day, keeping you from optimal brain performance (Ogawa, Kaizuma-Ueyama, and Hayashi, 2022). The best thing to do is to set your alarm to the last possible minute you can sleep and then just get up. Place your phone or alarm clock across the room so you have to get up to turn it off, and then go to another room and meditate for 12 minutes. Yep, meditate. Just feel your breath. Just feel your body breathe for you. There is a meditation challenge at the end of this chapter that gives you an easy way to get started. Instead of pressing snooze, take that snooze time and start to engage your frontal lobe so that you can have optimal brain performance, clarity, decisiveness, more empathy, and peace, just to name a few of the benefits.

When we start our day, sitting in our own silence, we are able to bring peace into our heart. We are then able to walk through life with that peace, making decisions aligned with peace and love. Our disposition is better, we can let things go, and we find that we respond to challenges instead of reacting to them. We have more empathy and compassion for others. We are more patient, more kind, and more understanding of the human experience, ourselves, and others.

If you are skeptical of this practice and thinking, "Nobody has time for this!" I am telling you, when you can bring meditation into your daily routine, you gain hours of time each day, because you start working smarter, not harder; you are more productive, more creative, and you access a flow state that carries you through all your days.

The 12 minutes in a chair is worth so much more than that non-sleep of a snooze button. And sometimes you may fall asleep while in your meditation chair, and that is ok, for there are only three things that can happen when you meditate: fall asleep, have thoughts, or just sit in your own stillness. There you go. The multi-million dollar suggestion that may actually make some of you multi-millionaires because you will become so creative and in your flow zone that who knows what you will come up with. And some of us may just stay in the classroom which is awesome as well, for our students need us. And our students need the best version of us. Do you know where that best version can be found? In our hearts. When we are in our stillness, we are able to tap into our hearts, align with the best version of ourselves, and decipher where our energy needs to go, who we need to engage with, and what we need to create.

When we then come into our classroom with a mind and heart cultivated and primed for the day with peace, only good things are possible. We owe it to ourselves and our students to spend time in silence. Once we do that, we are also more aware of what helps us tap into our own personal flourishing, and we can use that as resources and tools for when we feel a little wound up or overwhelmed.

We can learn to ground ourselves so that we can be there for others. If we are flourishing, our students will start to flourish just by being in our presence and positive energy. And we are better equipped to help students learn to tap into their flourishing. This is a super power my friends! If we can help our students tap into their own personal flourishing at such a young age, wow!, how life changing that will be! And really, we'll be able to help make this world a better place, one student at a time, one class at a time, as they learn to walk through life with peace.

We also need to make sure we are nourishing our body, mind, and spirit. What are you watching on tv or social media? What podcasts or news are you listening to? What foods are you putting into your body? All of those things contribute to your flourishing. Make sure it is worthy of your consumption.

Maybe you are just starting out on your own journey of flourishing and are not sure where to start. Go on a wellness retreat. Maybe a weekend away at the beach or in the mountains where you can get fresh air and be close to nature. Or make it as simple as going to spend some time in your local bookstore and find a book that speaks to you on personal growth. Turn off the news and build a garden like the album cover by Lukas Nelson and Promise of the Real. Or maybe it is as simple as going to bed early, limiting your alcohol and junk food consumption, and moving your body daily. We all have room for improvement, and those little things can help us realize where we may be lacking in our flourishing.

Back to meditation. There are so many benefits of meditation such as mental clarity, reversal of aging, being able to handle challenges, more joy, more energy, more productivity, ability to focus, better sleep, etc. Regarding mental wellness, meditation has been scientifically proven by neuroscientist Sara Lazar to shrink the amygdala, that part of the brain that holds anxiety, stress, and depression (McGreevey, 2011). When we take time to meditate, we send energy to the hippocampus part of our brain that holds memory, clarity, creativity, and the ability to tap into emotional intelligence. The more energy sent to the hippocampus, the less energy goes to the amygdala, which in turn shrinks.

This simple, yet profound, activity is still intimidating to some people. "But I can't meditate; I think too much!" (First of all, can't, scared and fear should be taken out of your vocabulary, but more on that in a bit.) The biggest misconception with meditation is that you have to stop thinking or clear your mind when you meditate. We have 60,000–80,000 thoughts a day, so telling your mind not to think is like telling your heart not to beat or lungs not to bring in air; it's impossible. Through meditation, we are learning how to see our thoughts, but let them pass by as if they were clouds. A Zen Monk named Suzuki once stated that when we meditate, we leave the front door and the back door of our mind open, so that thoughts can come in and go out; we just do not serve them tea (Mukesh, 2020). So, as we learn how to sit in our own stillness, we learn to become aware of our thoughts, but not pay them any energy.

To live a life full of abundance on all levels, we need to change the narrative that we have with ourselves. We need to always speak kindly to ourselves. We are spiritual beings having a human experience, and we need to be kind and gentle to ourselves. We need to love ourselves before we can love others, as well as, be our biggest cheerleader and advocate because let's face it, we are dealing with other humans who are suffering from their own inadequacies. We need to stop saying the words can't, scared, and fear. Why live in fear when you can live in love? Now I understand that some people are truly in dangerous situations and I am not being insensitive to them, in fact, I pray that they will find courage and the means to escape those situations and will heal and be able to live in love.

Once you remove those negative and condescending words from your vocabulary, you will be astonished at how quickly things change around you. My sister Holly Mirenda once said, "Fear and courage are the same energy, it is just what you name the emotion." Same with nervousness and excitement; it is the same energy. One name has a negative connotation and one has a positive one. Pick the positive one, always pick positive!

And while we are on words, please stop apologizing! Stop saying "I'm sorry." For what? Living? It belittles you. Yes, of course, there are times when we truly need to apologize for a wrong we have done, but walking down the street, or voicing your opinion in a conversation, or coming to an awkward moment with a stranger does not require those words that have lost their meaning and people tend to use as filler words. Stop saying it.

Instead try, "Thank you so much for waiting for me," "Excuse me," "This is what I think." Stop belittling yourself. Every time you apologize, you are asking permission from the other person to speak. You are a dynamic human being with the purpose to make this world a better place; never apologize for you!

Take negativity out of your vocabulary, even sarcasm. When we speak down about ourselves, our brain and body start to believe it and that is what you become. When we build ourselves up and say loving, positive things, our body hears that and responds and that is what we become. You are limitless! You can do anything! It will not happen overnight, but the kinder you are to yourself, the more you will become the person you want and are meant to be. Be kind to everyone, especially yourself! Choose your words carefully and you will see yourself flourish. Instead of "I can't do this" say "I am choosing this." Live in abundance, not scarcity. Choose your words to reflect abundance, and you will receive abundance. Everything is vibrational so what you put out there is what you attract. So keep your words positive, always, especially when talking about yourself. Just another small change that helps you flourish.

Be sure to manage your time wisely. Compartmentalize your day with your different responsibilities. When you walk into the school building, leave home at home; and when you walk into your home, leave school at school. We need to rest and recalibrate from the energies of both. Work during your school hours, staying late if you need to finish paperwork, grading, or a project; but try not to bring your work home. Home needs to be a sanctuary for you; a place of rejuvenation and a place of peace. When you are home, take off the teacher hat. Leave the school hat at school, so you can tend to and live the rest of your life consciously.

Mindfulness can help us heal our own bodies. The breath can heal. Allow it to heal you. The placebo effect is good and proof that mindfulness and optimism can heal. It works. We can heal ourselves. Heal yourself from adverse thoughts and ways.

Find out what makes you happy and do more of that. Do it whenever you can. If it brings you joy, do it!

How can you practice self-care today? Journal, paint, plant, laugh … the possibilities are endless. Do it; each and every day.

So essentially bringing mindfulness into the classroom starts with you. Foster your own self-love and peace and that will radiate from your being, into your space, and then have a ripple effect throughout the rest of the world.

 ## Try It! Take the Seven Day Teacher Meditation Challenge

Day 1

Challenge yourself to set your alarm for 15 minutes earlier, or if you press snooze, get up instead and drag yourself into another room. Sit in a chair for 5 minutes, 10 minutes, 15 minutes, however long you can allow yourself, and just feel your body breathe for you. Just Be and breathe. Notice how you are breathing. Are you breathing in and out of your nose? In and out of your mouth, or a combination of the two? Just feel your body breathe for you. Add a mantra/positive affirmation such as "All is well" or your own, and just breathe and Be. Repeat the mantra with each inhale or exhale of your breath. Make sure you set a timer on your phone to bring you out of the meditation if you have some place to be.

> Journal – How can I practice self-care today?
>
> As you are driving to work, or are in your own space, notice something that is of beauty.

Day 2

Set your alarm for 15 minutes earlier, or if you press snooze, get up instead and drag yourself into another room. Sit in a chair for 5 minutes, 10 minutes, 15 minutes, however long you can allow yourself, and just feel your body breathe for you. Just Be and breathe. Notice how you are breathing. Are you breathing in and out of your nose? In and out of your mouth, or a combination of the two? Just feel your body breathe for you. Bring to mind the most perfect vision for your life. Think about how this looks, how it feels in your heart, what it smells like, what it tastes like, what it sounds like. Feel yourself already there, in your perfect vision of your life. Feel it in your heart, your body; just Be in this vision. Bring to mind the mantra "I trust." Repeat the mantra with each inhale or exhale of your breath. Make sure you set a timer on your phone to bring you out of the meditation if you have some place to be.

> Journal – What is the perfect vision for my life? Where am I? What am I? Who am I? Who or what else is involved?
>
> Throughout today, come back to your breath. From time to time, just inhale deeply and exhale. Notice your breath and how you are breathing.

Day 3

Set your alarm for 15 minutes earlier, or if you press snooze, get up instead and drag yourself into another room. Sit in a chair for 5 minutes, 10 minutes, 15 minutes, however long you can allow yourself, and just feel your body breathe for you. Just Be and breathe. Notice how you are breathing. Are you breathing in and out of your nose? In and out of your mouth, or a combination of the two? Just feel your body breathe for you. Bring to mind all that you are grateful for. Make a list in your mind of all the simple things and big things. Bring to mind the mantra "Thank you." Repeat the mantra with each inhale or exhale of your breath. Make sure you set a timer on your phone to bring you out of the meditation if you have some place to be.

> Journal – Give gratitude for your life. Expand on the little and big things that you are grateful for.
>
> Instead of saying "I'm sorry" try saying "thank you" as you go about your day.

Day 4
Set your alarm for 15 minutes earlier, or if you press snooze, get up instead and drag yourself into another room. Sit in a chair for 5 minutes, 10 minutes, 15 minutes, however long you can allow yourself, and just feel your body breathe for you. Just Be and breathe. Notice how you are breathing. Are you breathing in and out of your nose? In and out of your mouth, or a combination of the two? Just feel your body breathe for you. Bring to mind the mantra "I am strong." Repeat the mantra with each inhale or exhale of your breath. Make sure you set a timer on your phone to bring you out of the meditation if you have some place to be.

> Journal – Write down all the qualities about yourself that you love or like. Expand on why.
>
> Smile all day long. Even if you don't feel like it, smile. Smiling releases endorphins throughout our body and adds to our well-being and mood.

Day 5

Set your alarm for 15 minutes earlier, or if you press snooze, get up instead and drag yourself into another room. Sit in a chair for 5 minutes, 10 minutes, 15 minutes, however long you can allow yourself, and just feel your body breathe for you. Just Be and breathe. Notice how you are breathing. Are you breathing in and out of your nose? In and out of your mouth, or a combination of the two? Just feel your body breathe for you. Spread your palms wide in your lap, on your knees, or by your side. When our hands are open we are in a receiving mode. What gifts are coming to you? What opportunities? What connections? What good is coming? Bring to mind the mantra "I am open." Repeat the mantra with each inhale or exhale of your breath. Make sure you set a timer on your phone to bring you out of the meditation if you have some place to be.

> Journal – What goals do you have for your life? What do you need to do to reach those goals? What is one thing you can do for today that puts you one step closer to those goals?
>
> As you walk through your day, say positive affirmations.

Day 6

Set your alarm for 15 minutes earlier, or if you press snooze, get up instead and drag yourself into another room. Sit in a chair for 5 minutes, 10 minutes, 15 minutes, however long you can allow yourself, and just feel your body breathe for you. Just Be and breathe. Notice how you are breathing. Are you breathing in and out of your nose? In and out of your mouth, or a combination of the two? Just feel your body breathe for you. Crawl into your heart and wrap it around you like the blanket of peace that it is. This place of solace and calm is available to you at any time of day. Just sit in your own peace and feel life being given to you through your breath. Bring to mind the mantra "I am love" and with each inhale or exhale of your breath, repeat these words silently in your mind and in your throat.

Journal – Where do you need to place your energy for today? Where do you want to place your energy? Where can you find balance?

As you go about your day, when you find you are becoming distracted, bring your awareness back to the task at hand, or your breath.

Day 7

Set your alarm for 15 minutes earlier, or if you press snooze, get up instead and drag yourself into another room. Sit in a chair for 5 minutes, 10 minutes, 15 minutes, however long you can allow yourself, and just feel your body breathe for you. Just Be and breathe. Notice how you are breathing. Are you breathing in and out of your nose? In and out of your mouth, or a combination of the two? Just feel your body breathe for you. Crawl into your heart and wrap it around you like the blanket of peace that it is. This place of solace and calm is available to you at any time of day. Grant yourself grace. Know that goals and visions do not happen overnight. Have patience and trust in the process. Just Be and breathe. Bring to mind the mantra "I am peace, I am love, I am light" and with each inhale or exhale of breath, repeat those words silently in your mind and in your throat.

Journal – I am peace, I am love, I am light. How are you each? How can you be even more so?

Be aware of how you are peace, love, and light to others throughout your day today.

Further Resources on Meditation

◆ I offer Zoom sessions that can help support your meditation journey as an educator or parent, whether you are a beginner or a professional. You can sign up on my website at www.innerlightwellness.online and I look forward to assisting you in accessing the tools to walk your own path of peace, thus assisting others to do the same.

◆ I also have free meditations on the Insight Timer App that deal with a variety of topics to help ease stress and bring peace into your heart.

◆ Get certified in meditation through Unplug Meditation Teacher Training. This great program will help you find your own inner peace, even if you decide not to become a meditation coach.

References

McGreevey, Sue. "Eight Weeks to a Better Brain". *The Harvard Gazette*. January 21, 2011. https://news.harvard.edu/gazette/story/2011/01/eight-weeks-to-a-better-brain/

Mukesh, Mani. "25 Insightful Shunryū Suzuki Quotes On Life, Zazen and More (With Meaning)". OutofStress. October 4, 2020. https://www.outofstress.com/zen-monk-shunryu-suzuki-quotes/.

Ogawa, K., Kaizuma-Ueyama, E. & Hayashi, M. "Effects of using a snooze alarm on sleep inertia after morning awakening". *J Physiol Anthropol* 41, 43 (2022). https://doi.org/10.1186/s40101-022-00317-w

3

Mindfulness for Student Anxiety and Redirecting

As adults, we have felt anxiety in social situations; going to a party where you do not know anyone, attending a business trip to network with new people, attending a conference where you know you'll have ice breakers. All of these situations produce some level of anxiety in adults, but we have learned to rely on our self-confidence and know all will be ok and maybe even fun.

Our children have these same feelings, but they are new, and they do not know how to handle them. They can be overwhelming, and we as teachers and parents need to be careful not to put too much pressure on them and instead, give them a safe space to express their concerns. It is important that their feelings are validated, which helps them feel seen, and in control. It also gives them the confidence to share their truth moving forward.

We can teach our children tools to calm themselves and give them confidence to move through life knowing that All Is Well. Once children have these tools, they can self soothe instead of reaching for things that numb later in life. They can then have confidence to interact with others, to play, collaborate, and create.

A child who has self-confidence can do anything with their life that they want. They can be successful in all the ways that are important to them. They can help make this world a better place by spreading kindness, charity, and love. They find value in

DOI: 10.4324/9781003511847-3

taking care of themselves, others, and our world. The earlier that one gains self-confidence, the earlier they can tap into self-love, which can change the trajectory of their life.

It takes some people a lifetime to learn to not worry about other people's judgments. But if children can learn from a young age to love themselves, embrace who they are, and continue to evolve into the next best version of themselves, it can only help make our planet a more peaceful place.

It is like the shedding of the snakeskin. We are meant to evolve into a better version of ourselves throughout our life. Learning to love oneself, having confidence, and aligning with love allow us to live life with less anxiety, for we are more present and mindful of our world and the beauty that surrounds us. When we are conscious of our life, we recognize the good in the world and become problem solvers and want to help others experience a world that is full of good.

We are all still going to have social anxiety from time to time as it is part of the human experience. But the sooner we learn tools such as deep breathing, noticing and feeling our breath, and positive affirmations, the easier it is to walk through life with peace in our heart. This is important so that children can bring peace to others with their positive energy. We want children to thrive and flourish, so that our world can take one-step closer to peace, one conscious being at a time.

As parents and educators, we are providing what is necessary for students to learn how to walk through life. Breathing and positive affirmations can help all students, not only those with anxiety. It is necessary so that students can access their own peace at any time of day. Only then can one learn how to use these tools to be successful on their own.

When your student or child is dealing with social anxiety, remind them that it is normal to feel that way. Be kind and think about when you were a child and how you would feel if you had these fears. Align yourself with love. Do not get frustrated. This is your child, and their feelings are real. Let them know you love them and care about them. Let them know you are there for them no matter what. Let them know that their feelings are valid. Help them breathe. Remind them of positive affirmations. A list can be at the end of this chapter. Your love will help guide them to their heart and their peace.

One way to help ease students' social anxiety is to bring mindfulness into the daily classroom routine. It takes less than 10 minutes. But in order to have buy-in from students, we have to be building a rapport, or already have a rapport established. The beauty of bringing mindfulness into your classroom is that you are setting up opportunities to build a community and culture of trust within your classroom. Students will feel safe; safe with each other, safe with you, safe with themselves. Everyone is doing the work together; weaving a blanket of peace that only ripples out into the school, community, and world.

Mindfulness can also help us all become better at focusing. Our students' attention spans are super short these days, especially with the amount of time we all spend on technology. Mindfulness teaches our brains to focus, as we develop the ability to attend to a task such as feeling our breath during meditation/mindfulness or bringing our awareness to our positive affirmation while we meditate or are mindful. One of those 60,000 to 80,000 thoughts that we think each day pops into our head, but we let it pass by as if it was a cloud, and we bring our awareness back to our breath or our positive affirmation. The more we practice mindfulness throughout our days, the more we are able to do the same outside of meditation/mindfulness, for we are building focusing stamina as well as the capacity to return to the task at hand and let the thoughts roll by. So, when we are doing a task, whether that is school work, a project, our own work, we have our thoughts, but can quickly bring our awareness back to the task in front of us.

We are actually cultivating optimum brain performance. We are bringing about acute sharpness of mind and clarity. We are staying sharp and attentive. We are becoming conscious. Making conscious decisions.

When we can teach our children at a young age, really any age, to become mindful, feeling their breath, saying positive affirmations, they then take that into the classroom where they can apply it to their assignment or assessment. When they become distracted by a thought, they can recognize that thought, let it pass by as if it is a cloud, and gently bring themselves back to the task in front of them. They can do this with grace and compassion for themselves, realizing that thoughts are just part of living and creating.

Learning to breathe mindfully, and taking time to breathe, also helps control anxiety which goes along with attention problems. When we can calm our breath, we are able to calm our bodies, bringing our blood pressure down and reducing the need for flight or fight.

Mindfulness makes students better prepared for their day because they are conscious of their decisions and actions. Being able to be mindful brings about self-confidence, thus allowing students to collaborate with others, and create.

Students with attention issues actually have the ability to be better learners and problem solvers because they have to overcompensate for their lack of attention span. They can learn strategies to survive in the academic world and life, mindfulness being one of them. People with attention issues are some of our greatest creators, game changers, and developers of new ideas and concepts. Embrace the gift and learn to manage it, spending time in silence and listening to your heart through mindfulness.

You will find at the back of this book a *Thirty Day Classroom Mindfulness Challenge* already written for you, with precise things to do each day that will allow you to use less than 10 minutes of your day to foster a classroom of peace. If you start this at the beginning of the year, you will establish mindfulness routines that will last the entire year, and really, into life. If you start at any other point in the year, you will still see the benefits.

Mindfulness is as simple as just becoming aware. Aware of your surroundings, aware of your body, aware of your breath. When you are noticing this moment, and consciously feeling how your body breaths, that is being mindful. When you are noticing the moment and bring your attention to something such as leaves blowing in the wind, the sounds of birds singing, the smile of a child, that is mindfulness. We do not have to sit in a semi lotus position with Zen music playing in the background to be mindful. We just need to consciously be aware of our surroundings and notice.

Try It: Activities to Teach Students to Be Mindful and Grounded in the Present

These can be done anywhere (car, office chair, while waiting in line):

1. Feel Your Breath: Sit in a comfortable position. Take a long slow deep breath in through the nose as if you are smelling flowers; then exhale that breath out of your mouth as if you are blowing out a candle. Repeat this three times, and then breathe normal, whatever that means to you. Notice how you breathe without trying. Do you breathe in and out of your mouth? In and out of your nose? Or a combination of the two? Feel your breath, and how it enters and exits your body. Just notice.

2. Mindful Hands: Place your pointer finder at the base of your palm, above your wrist. Take a deep breath in and move your pointer finger up to the tip of your thumb. As you exhale, move your pointer finger back down to the base of your palm. With your next breath in, move your finger up to the tip of your pointer finger, and as you exhale, bring the finger back to the base of your palm. Inhale again and move your finger up to the tip of your middle finger; and as you exhale, bring the finger down to the base of the palm. Breath in, moving your finger to the tip of the ring finger, and as you exhale, bring your finger back to the base of your palm. Inhale, finger goes to the tip of your index finger, and as you exhale, finger moves back to the base of the palm.

3. Setting Intentions: What is it that you want for your day? For your week? Month? Year? Life? Plant seeds of intentions to help guide you toward your purpose.

4. Essential Oils: Use essential oils in your classroom through a diffuser. The steam puts out a scent that can invigorate or calm the room depending on what oil you choose to use.

5. The Use of Sound: Use a sound to indicate transitions. A triangle, a Koshi chime, a mini gong, a Tibetan bowl, whatever you are drawn to that makes a pleasant sound

6. Have a positive affirmation on your board always. Change it up as you see fit. Just reading it to themselves, on their own time, helps students to keep it in their mind throughout the day, and teaches them to use positive affirmations throughout their life when faced with challenges and uncertainty. Some positive affirmations to use:

I am love.	I am kind.	I am light.
I am strong.	Thank you.	I am thoughtful.
I am brave.	I can do anything.	I am a helper.
I am creative.	I am loved.	I am calm.
I am a good friend.	I am peace.	I am safe.
I am open.	I am resilient.	I am the best me.

   Talk about what these words mean. Brainstorm what this positive affirmation means. Have students give their feedback on what it means to them.

7. Use simple yoga poses for brain breaks or when you need to bring some energy into your classroom. Pick a pose and have everyone do it as they breathe through the pose, noticing their body, their strength, and their breath as they breathe in through their nose, and exhale out of their mouth. Some examples and illustrations of poses are shown on the following page.

8. Use Global Tinker Mini Meditations for Kids on YouTube and wherever podcasts are found. This is my collaborative project with Global Tinker that was voted one of The Best Podcasts for Children for 2022 and 2023 by Common Sense Media. My Mini Meditations for Kids average about 5 minutes and deal with specific issues such as anxiety, taking a test, and dealing with a bully. A link to the animated version and the podcast version can be found at www.bringingmindfulnessintotheclassroom.com

9. Better yet, have a Mindfulness composition book where students can journal, draw, include their gratitude lists, quotes, etc.

10. Take a moment in your class to allow students to just feel their body breathe for them. Here is a simple meditation that can be adapted to your style and affirmation. Make sure you pause throughout to allow students to tap into their heart and calm themselves.

Start by getting comfortable sitting on the floor or chair.

Close your eyes if you wish, or just rest your gaze on the floor below, or ceiling, or sky above.

Feel free to change position if necessary during our mindfulness time.

Begin by taking a long, slow, deep breath in through your nose, and gently exhale that breath out of your mouth.

Again, take another long slow deep breath in through your nose, and gently exhale out of your mouth.

Now just feel your body breathing normally for you, without you trying to force your breath.

Just let your body breathe naturally and notice your breath.
How is your body breathing for you?
Are you breathing in and out of your nose, in and out of your mouth, or a combination of the two?
Just feel your body breathing, and notice your breath for a few moments.
Let us repeat the words (positive affirmation said here) silently in our mind, and in our throat with each inhale or exhale of our breath.
Silently say (positive affirmation) with each breath.
Take a long slow deep breath in through your nose, and slowly exhale out of your mouth.
With your eyes still closed, become aware of your surroundings, how your body feels, how you are breathing now.
When you are ready, open your eyes.

11. Bring art into your lessons through painting, drawing, music, movement, dance, and theater. Art and learning in a new way, or proving what they have learned in a new way, allows one to be mindful in their task. They also may discover a new form of creativity that they did not realize they enjoy.

12. Writing a thank you card/letter. This simple act of gratitude not only fills your heart, but brings a smile to someone else's face, allowing the ripple effect of our positive actions to flow to other human beings in ways we will never know.

13. Have students research a positive quote that resonates with them and then write about the connection. Put the quote on the board. Draw names from a jar to determine which quote you are posting. This can be done anonymously or not, and then post daily, weekly, however you see fit. Allow students to be artistic with their quote. Students could even talk about their connection if you are working on a speaking and listening standard, or the quote could just be written for all to see.

14. Gratitude journals are so helpful in realizing the beauty in the simple things in life. When we have gratitude in our hearts, we notice the good in our days, even if it is something small, and learn to appreciate the small and

big things in life. It also fills our heart with love. Journals can be used to create images, words, sentences, and/or full entries. It is up to the owner.

15. Create a Mindfulness Corner. Place a rug, a positive quote, a plant, a light, streamers, a bean bag, yoga mats, anything that speaks to you as a place to sit and just Be. This will also be a good indicator that you may need to check in with students who use it or not, but just having this little spot gives the opportunity to go within even in a chaotic class. You will have to see what works for your class. Even if you do not have a spot in your class, see if your school will offer a room, or a space. It could be a Zen room, chill out room, whatever your school culture calls for.

    Even in your own home, find a small space where you can go within and just be. Add a festive pillow, plant, books, rocks, whatever brings you tiny joys, to surround yourself with as you meditate.

16. Give the opportunity for students to connect to music by either making it with real instruments or a program that allows them to make their own electronic beats.

17. Blowing Bubbles helps children start to understand their breath and become mindful in their breathing. It is also a soothing way to take a moment and discover the simple joys in life.

18. Windchimes are a lovely way to become mindful. Hearing the beautiful vibrations of notes can immediately soothe. Take a moment to just listen, and breathe.

19. Make a Glitter Tube – Any cylinder or jar works. Add clear glue, water, glitter, and beads to the cylinder. Screw the top on tight. Shake up the tube and watch the glitter and beads swirl around. After making the craft, have students shake up their tube and notice the swirling of the contents. Have them close their eyes and feel their breath for a few minutes. Add a positive affirmation and continue to breathe. When they are finished with the breathing exercise, have them notice how the glitter tube settled, just like their thoughts when they were mindful of their breath.

Try It: Mindful Activities to Reduce Student Anxiety

1. When someone is nervous, bring out a positive affirmation such as "All is Well," "Only Good Lies Ahead," and "I am Loved." Validate the child's feelings and make a connection to when you once felt that way. Then give them that positive affirmation to use to calm.

2. Tapping is a great way to get rid of anxiety and be mindful. Michele Capots, a transformational coach for mental wellness and resilience says,

   > Emotional Freedom Technique (EFT), more commonly known as tapping, is a stress reduction tool that balances the energy systems of the body. It has often been referred to as psychological acupuncture because it uses the fingertips, instead of needles, on the meridian points found in Chinese medicine. EFT is widely being used by medical and mental health professionals, by athletes, and also in the education system. Research has shown when used in the classroom, tapping decreases students' test anxiety, increases concentration, and also promotes creativity. Even the simple combination of tapping on the body with the breath can be used as an emotional regulation tool to ground someone and bring them back to their body, especially during a crisis.

3. Tapping between the ring and pinkie finger can bring relief to anxious moments, along with the temples and collarbone.

4. Spend time with your students or child just breathing. Breath together, feeling and noticing your breath.

5. The act of doodling is cathartic. Use it as a brain break, or use it as a way to wrap up your lesson. What can they draw to represent what they learned?

6. Use background music in your class or home that is set to a higher vibrational frequency such as Mind Castle. The beautiful nature videos that accompany the music are

found on YouTube. Or find lyric-less music that you find calming such as classical music or beats and play it in the background of the class while students are working independently.

7. Spending time with a pet is so healing. Animals are so healing. They sense our energy and emotions, and can help us feel better when we are down, and bring joy to our lives. Even if you do not have a pet of your own, consider volunteering at an animal shelter, or have therapy dogs come to your school.

8. Release Ceremony: Write down a list of things that are bothering you and then rip up the list. Make peace with the fact that you are no longer worrying about those things and are living in the present. This is a great way to start off the day, as students come into the classroom with their potential baggage, and this activity allows them to let it all go and enjoy their day at school.

Further Resources on Mindfulness

♦   Books that support mindfulness in other arenas of life:
    Fire Child, Water Child by Stephen Scott Cowan, MD
    Super Me by Adi Benning
    The Paper Girls Show Orgami Craft Book: 21 Folding Creations by Global Tinker

♦   To bring professional developments for teachers, assemblies for students, and/or workshops for parents to your school, inquire at www.bringingmindfulnessintotheclass room.com

4

Mindfulness for Student Strengths and Collaboration

Think of individuals as spices. They are a variety of spices combined with other spices making their own seasonal blend of uniqueness to add flavor to our world. No two students are the same. We all come from different backgrounds, cultures, experiences, and that makes us who we are. We need to accept each other for our uniqueness and see it as a way to enhance our world and to learn new ways of doing things and new ways of experiencing life. One person's way of living is not necessarily going to be your way of living, but allowing people to be individuals and live according to what makes them happy is important to one's quality of life.

How boring life would be if everyone was the same. Embrace your child or student's uniqueness for that is what is going to make them successful, a creator, a problem solver, and world changer. Allow your students to be who they are and teach to their strengths. How do they learn best according to their uniqueness? What are they interested in? Teaching to their strengths and interests also validates who they are, thus giving them self-confidence and fosters a joy in learning.

Embracing individuality also fosters a safe climate in the classroom where students feel that they can be themselves and share their joys, challenges, and triumphs. This weaves a blanket

DOI: 10.4324/9781003511847-4

of peace amongst students, your classroom, the school, and the community, as students feel connected.

Students also need to look within to find out what brings them joy, where their interests lie, and to know their strengths. Once they have found these insights, they then develop the confidence to collaborate with others and create. Even preschoolers revel in happiness and joy when they make new discoveries. This is what we should be doing in our classrooms every day; giving students the opportunity to become curious, look within and determine their feelings, their celebrations, their joy.

When we give students the opportunity to spend a few moments in class to gather their thoughts, or to just be, our classroom develops an energy of peace, safety, and a connection between the individuals who reside within those walls. Not only does that calmness stay within those walls, it is also carried out into the world as those students step beyond the classroom, for they are coming to know who they are, what their strengths are and are determining their purpose in the world. When they know what contributes to their flourishing, they learn to recognize the abundance in their lives and their own resiliency. Their strengths become more apparent, and their self-confidence only grows as they begin to believe in themselves.

Flourishing is the ability to thrive in life, to find joy in the everyday and to know you are living with purpose. When we understand what it is that brings us true joy, then we can turn to those things to better know ourselves and our strengths, as well as turn to those joy makers when we are feeling stressed or overwhelmed. When we know our strengths, we become more confident in ourselves and are then able to collaborate with others and create. We want to teach our students the same thing. We want to give them access to understanding themselves on a level other than academia, and we want this to unfold organically in the classroom by incorporating flourishing and mindfulness into our curriculum.

To do this, we need to build rapport with our students. We need to set the energy in our classroom as a positive, safe, and nurturing environment. Through discovering ourselves, we can then help others to do the same, mainly our students. When we allow students to tap into themselves and foster a culture of flourishing within our classroom, the possibilities are endless.

Changing the language we use in the classroom to one of success and accomplishment needs to be administered from day one. Taking out words such as can't, too hard, and difficult and replacing them with success, challenge, and brain exercise create an achieving and performance mindset that fosters the possibility of accomplishment for all students. Students then gain self-confidence, are then able to collaborate fully with others, and create.

We communicate in different ways. Our body language tells just as much of a story as our voice. The tone we use indicates how we are feeling at the time. When we learn ways to tap into our inner strength and gain confidence, we carry ourselves differently and speak more assertively, yet still with kindness.

Try It: Ways to Use Mindfulness to Teach Student Strengths and Build Rapport

This is not something extra that is a burden to educators, but a conscious awareness to merge together curriculum and mindfulness; a new way of teaching that develops rapport and a culture of acceptance and harmony within your classroom.

These questions are a great way to open up the school year and move through the school year. I know as educators we get so busy fitting everything into our lesson plans, to stay on pace with the other teachers in our department. Use these moments to connect with students throughout the year, as time allows. Again, this is not something extra. This is something, when completed over time, gives a richer classroom environment and fosters higher level thinking and creating. As students discover their strengths, they build confidence around those strengths and then can collaborate with others and create.

Questions to Guide Personal Flourishing

- ◆ Write down three things that make you smile.
- ◆ Write down a challenge that you enjoy.
- ◆ Write down something you are proud of.

- ◆ If you could do anything with your life, what would it be?
- ◆ Where would you live?
- ◆ Where would you travel?
- ◆ What is your idea of a perfect weekend?
- ◆ Who is one successful person you admire and why?
- ◆ How would you serve others?
- ◆ If you had $1,000 to give to any non-profit charity, which one would you choose and why?
- ◆ Write down three people who impacted your life?
- ◆ What goal are you working on right now or would like to make?
- ◆ What would you like people to know about you?
- ◆ What is your wish for your life?
- ◆ What can you do to make this world a better place?
- ◆ How can you practice self-care?
- ◆ What does Peace mean to me?
- ◆ How can I be a better friend?

Give students time to write, or opportunities to discuss their dreams and/or what makes them tick.

Have a round table discussion from one of the questions to stimulate conscious awareness of the students, aka mindfulness.

Incorporate a question or two into a Socratic Seminar.

Journals – daily or weekly journals help to set classroom routines, calm the students, help them to become better writers, and also to learn more about the person they are and the person they are becoming. Use questions above or have them connect with text or other mediums.

Come up with your own journal according to the news of your students, as you get to know them better. Help them to navigate life, to navigate the challenges they are facing with grace and with peace, as you give them the opportunity to become creative in their response in a peaceful manner.

Use these moments to connect with students throughout the year, as time allows. When completed over time, these questions add to a richer classroom environment and fosters higher level thinking and creating. As students discover their strengths, they build confidence around those strengths, and then can collaborate with others and create.

Other Mindful Activities to Help Students Find Their Strengths

Show and Tell teaches children to find and use their voice as well as discover what they enjoy and what makes them unique. Listening and speaking skills are a must in our world, and this practice allows students to learn to be respectful toward others.

Vision Boards with old school magazines, or electronically with google slides and images from the web can act as a way to dream and create. I like to start out the year with a lesson called *Snippet Of Me* in which students create their own slide with pictures that represent themselves, quotes, or words. It allows students to describe who they are visually.

Use Visualization to help students be successful. Have them see themselves doing great on a test, knowing all the answers, and finding it easy. Students have learned all the material, it is all in their brain, they just need to retrieve it. By visualizing their success, they bring their awareness to that hippocampus part of their brain to access the information. With any act of life that requires performance, have students visualize the best case scenario and their top performance.

Collaborate with Your Art Teacher or art department and allow students to design and paint murals that display images or words reminding students to be mindful and/or accept their uniqueness and diversity.

Journaling is a great practice for students of all ages to get their thoughts on paper and discover something new about themselves. Preschoolers can draw pictures instead of writing sentences.

Journal Prompts:

◆ What can I do to make this world a better place?
◆ What am I grateful for?

- ◆ If I had $1,000 to give to a non-profit organization, who would I give it to and why?
- ◆ If I could travel anywhere in the world, where would it be and why? What would I do there? Who would I take? What would I bring back? How long would I stay?
- ◆ What would be my dream job?
- ◆ What is your idea of a perfect summer?

After students have answered these prompts and others, they can put together a mini memoir of their work that shows things that are important to them, to better understand themselves, their values, their purpose, and direction.

Ways to Build Rapport with Your Students

Building rapport can be done as an entire class, but connections are established quicker when you can have one on one conversations with students. I suggest standing at your classroom door before class begins, saying hello to each student, and addressing them by name. As they enter the room, you can also pick up on their energy, their body language, their smile or lack of, and can make mental notes about your students and where some extra attention may need to be placed according to their dispositions.

Some ways to gain daily insight into your students and quickly build rapport:

- ◆ Ask students about their weekend/break.
- ◆ Ask about one of the many journaling questions above.
- ◆ Fist bump your students as they enter the classroom.
- ◆ Attend school events where your students are active such as a game, play, performance, etc.
- ◆ Ask about their routines and interests such their job, show, band, responsibilities, etc.
- ◆ Take requests and play their favorite song, game, quote, etc.
- ◆ Anything that connects you to your student, and makes them feel valued, and validated, do more of those things.

Ways to Have Students Collaborate

Collaboration builds rapport amongst students and helps them to problem solve and create. Students can be grouped according to friends, post it note colors, a playing card suit, an index card color, shoe color, or according to support levels of peers. I will hand out post it notes or index cards of different colors as students walk in the classroom, and then they are randomly grouped. Placing desks in groups and having students pick where they want to sit allows for autonomy. If started at the beginning of a semester, collaboration is always successful and only becomes more advantageous. Some examples are listed below to get your students collaborating from day one.

Easy ways for students to collaborate:

◆ What is a challenge you would like to solve in our school?
◆ What is a challenge you would like to solve in our community?
◆ What is a challenge you would like to solve in our world?
◆ Have your students collaborate on a video project documenting interviews of peers or school staff, nature, announcements, school news, etc.
◆ Use collaboration as a form of alternative assessments.
◆ Projects that require collaboration foster intellectual, emotional, and social growth as well as peer support through the rigor of a challenge. Find opportunities throughout your day to have students collaborate.

Further Resources on Flourishing

If you would like more information on flourishing and to see a ton of research that has been done, check out The Human Flourishing Program at Harvard's Institute for Quantitative Social Science: Community of Practice.

5

Mindfulness to Engage Students in Learning

When a student asks, "why do I need to know this?" it is not to learn facts, it is not to learn historical dates, or science necessarily, or calculus. The reason we need to know this is to learn how to expand our mind and think critically in the present, as well as in the future. When we are learning new concepts, we are building new synapses in our brain. When we are learning new things at school, we are expanding our mind and becoming more open, and being open to other schools of thought and ways of learning helps us to become smarter. Not necessarily book smart, but to learn in new ways.

Maybe later in life you are learning a new language or instrument, and you may not be aware that you are tapping back into the same synapses that you built when you were learning algebra, but your brain is able to learn in an easier manner because you already had those synapses built from when you were younger. The point of education is that students are learning how to learn in different ways which allows you to later in life collaborate and create in an easier manner with others, as well as problem solve and develop new skill sets.

When we foster a culture in our classroom of mindfulness, students become more engaged in the learning process. They ask questions. They want to have discussions to understand more thoroughly. We all learn differently. Some people are

DOI: 10.4324/9781003511847-5

visual learners taking in what is shown to them through videos and pictures. Some of us learn best through hearing information through lectures, podcasts, and conversations. Some learn through actually doing and having experiences. Some people learn a language best by being dropped off in that town and survive to have their basic needs met. Others learn a language by reading a book in that language or through the Duolingo App. Others by just sitting at a table and listening. Those synapses start going again and what we learned as a child starts to come into play and we are able to pick up a new language because we formed those synapses as we were younger learning how to solve formulas.

Teaching a classroom to all the different styles is a daily challenge, yet one we signed up to do as educators. As we teach these different styles, we are connecting with each student according to how they learn, and give them the ability to find success in academics. Drawing, painting, and art, in general, are forms of learning as well, as is music. Students learn through all forms of art and granting them access sets them up to be lifelong learners as they want to continue learning and become curious because they have had success through various forms of learning. They gain confidence in their ability to learn, no matter what the content may be and that fosters curiosity and the love of learning.

And maybe they don't show that love of learning right away because maybe they are distracted by TikTok and their social life, or just trying to have their basic needs met; but eventually it will come back. Eventually they will realize how learning opens doors and opportunities.

Just like with academics, when students or teachers ask, "Why do I need to learn mindfulness?" it is to set up habits to foster internal peace throughout one's lifetime, including the ripple effect of that peace that goes out to others and our world.

Puzzle Pieces Analogy

Whenever students are learning a new unit, it can seem daunting to those who struggle academically or are just not interested in the subject matter. I always use the puzzle analogy when introducing something new to my students. Each new unit is like a box of puzzle pieces. We dump out the puzzle pieces and get to work, putting the pieces together; finding where they fit, and slowly but surely, start to see the big picture. I remind students to give themselves grace, and have patience, for this is new material that they are comprehending for the first time. Allow the teacher to help guide you toward understanding. Allow yourself to question. Allow yourself to learn through the struggle, and then feel proud when you can prove what you have learned.

This analogy seems to ease the anxiety of learning for some students. It makes learning more attainable and gives them confidence in knowing that they will figure it out, even though it may be challenging.

Try It: Here Are Some Connections You Can Make between Mindfulness and the Subject You Are Teaching

Students will often ask why they are learning something; when will they use it in the future. Tie your curriculum to real world connections and then ask the students if that is something they are interested in doing in the future. Have them answer that question as a warmup, journal, or exit ticket. You can do this across any lesson and/or subject matter.

Independent Reading – Give students the autonomy to choose their own nonfiction or fictional book from your media center or classroom library, and give them 10 minutes to just read what interests them. This helps foster the love of reading but also allows students to just sit in their own silence and calm, which is welcoming during the busy school year. When your students are reading a required novel, incorporate independent reading so that they can stay on their reading schedule.

English – Have students identify themselves with a picture, quote, a color, music, poetry; any vignette.

Have students write their own quote, their own positive affirmation.

Social Studies – Connections! The history of us. What is our family history? Where did we come from? What were our ancestors' potential challenges, celebrations, and dreams?

Have students research someone from History that they respect, even recent history. See what words of wisdom they said and have them connect and write about one of the things said. What does it mean to them? What does it make them think about? How does it make them want to live their life?

Physical Education – How does movement make you feel? How does that exertion on your body make you feel? As educators, we honor the different responses and meet our students where they are to help them slowly build up a life of physical health, according to their interests and strengths.

Music – Students can identify themselves through music. Allow them to find a piece of music they relate to and discuss why. Or use lyrics to describe a character, time period in history, changes, etc.

Art – Students can identify themselves through art. They can make connections with different mediums. Allow students to be drawn toward certain types of art pieces or create their own. Artful Thinking can be done across curriculums, where students ponder what the art piece may mean through what they see, what they think, what they question, the connections they make, and potential themes of the art piece.

Foreign Languages – Journal entries, narratives, connections, etc…

Math – Have students play with numbers, find connections within numbers, and have the freedom to experiment and find patterns. Even something as simple as a number search can bring them into a mindful state and start to recognize sequences. Discuss number patterns in nature to show how numbers are everywhere.

Technology – Recognizing the patterns and sequences of coding, creating, editing, building. Remind students to bring their awareness to the task at hand, finding the beauty in their creation.

Science – Our entire planet is built upon the miracles of life and science; the possibilities of becoming aware of our world we are learning and exploring are endless. Simply bringing awareness to the beauty and awe of our world, space, physiology, chemistry, physics, and pondering these life forces can be an act of mindfulness. Break the curriculum down to the simplest unit, the simplest cell if you will, and build upon the amazing miracle of creation from there.

Essentially, it's about finding relevancy outside of the curriculum.

6

Mindfulness in Nature

Grounding

We become anxious, overwhelmed, indecisive, and scatterbrained when we are not grounded. We are unable to make decisions because there is too much going on in our head. There are a number of ways to ground yourself but the easiest and quickest is to go outside and breathe in fresh air. Take a walk, hike through the woods, or just stand on grass in your bare feet to allow roots to grow from your sciatic nerve and continue down into the earth. Allow Mother Earth to hold you and support you and give you everything you need. Place your palm on a tree and exchange your energy. Positive energy comes up from the earth and fills your body. Place your back against a tree to heal pain. Hug a tree.

There is a synchronistic perfection of life with the breath exchange between trees and humans; carbon dioxide and oxygen. If you can imagine a tree at twilight and a human lung x-ray, they look the same: bronchial tubes and alveoli; branches and leaves. We breathe in oxygen from the trees, and exhale carbon dioxide. The trees breathe in carbon dioxide, and exhale oxygen. Perfect synchronicity of life.

Meditation can help with grounding. Spend time in nature just being mindful. Smell the world around you as you breathe. Notice the wind on your arms, a sunbeam on your face. Just sit on the earth, lean against a tree, or be held by the healing waters as you float somewhere in nature. Be held by the sea. It is soothing

DOI: 10.4324/9781003511847-6

and healing. Salt from the sea or ocean will heal. The ocean can heal everything. If you don't have that luxury, a pool, river, lake, or even a bathtub can help. Be held by the waters.

Take your class outside and allow nature to calm them. Allow them to breathe in the fresh air and be calmed by nature. You may find they even become inspired. It is not necessary to move around once you are outside; just sitting and being is all that is required.

Physical activity is a great way to be mindful as well though so go on something as simple as a mindful nature walk. Feeling the foot touch the ground. Heel first, rounding to the tip of the toe. Standing up straight and walking. Noticing the breath as you walk. Noticing the birds and their song. Listening to the cicadas, looking at the vibrant colors of the flowers or leaves; adding whatever you become mindful of as you walk. Mindful walks can incorporate all forms of nature along the path. What can you find in the clouds?

We need to remember that each child is a human being, learning how to navigate this world. We are spiritual beings having a human experience. Our world is dictated by different energies including the five elements of fire, earth, metal, water, wood. We all have those energies inside of us and they dictate how we learn, communicate, and live life, as some are stronger than others. This is why we all do not fit into a square peg. We are all different shapes and sizes; some of us are triangles, circles, rhombuses, etc… This is what makes our world so beautiful for we are all so unique and came to create beautiful things for this earth. When we embrace our diversity and uniqueness, we are filled with joy and peace, for we have confidence in who we are. Allow yourself and your students to find the beauty in nature.

Try It! Activities for Getting Students Out into Nature

Five Senses Poem

A favorite activity at any age is to take the class outside with a clipboard, paper, and pencil. Have them write down something they see, something they hear, something they feel, something they taste, and something they smell. Have them use those words to describe something in nature or a feeling of just being in that moment. Allow students to write their poem while still outside to continue to be inspired. There are no rules to the poem structure. Allow students to be creative and express themselves however they wish.

Outdoor Nook

Talk to your school about building an outdoor classroom or nook. Connecting with nature is a lovely way to be mindful. A *Chill Room* or *Mindfulness Room* can also help students who need to diffuse or have a quiet space.

Nature Walk

Notice the beauty of our earth. Take a walk and watch the birds, trees, and/or clouds. Notice how the world is just living. Everything is just living.

Plant a Garden

This is as simple as starting with seeds on a windowsill, in solo cups, that your students plant; or actually plant outside. Students can set intentions for themselves as they plant the seed. What is something they want to grow in their life metaphorically? What is something that they want to see in their life? If your school allows for it, plant a community garden where the food can then be used in the cafeteria to have students taste the fruits of their labor, all while teaching them how to eat healthily.

At One with Nature

Directions for Students: Place your palm on the trunk of a tree. Notice how it feels. With your palm still on the tree, look up as high as you can to the top leaves and branches, and then work your eyesight down to each limb, all the way to your hand. Switch hands and repeat.

Field Trips

There is so much to see in our world! Take a field trip, if possible, to an arboretum, hiking trail, body of water, beach, etc… to study the land, plants, and animals. Students can become mindful scientists and learn about our world while experiencing its beauty.

7

How Teachers Can Help Parents with Mindfulness at Home

This section is framed with advice to include in a weekly or monthly email/newsletter that can remind parents of how to bring these strategies into their home while embracing their child's uniqueness. The chapter is written as if speaking to parents but can be adapted for a home/school connection.

The first thing we need to do is remind parents to embrace their children for who they are. Allow them to grow and unfold into the human being they are meant to be. Allow them to discover and explore and have their interests, not the parent's. It is easy to fall into the trap of wanting to push our children into pursuing our own dreams… being the star soccer player, the pianist, chemist, the ballerina, or quarterback. We want our children to be like who we were, but they have their own path to walk, and we need to respect that so that they can have confidence in who they are.

Confidence is one of the foundations of flourishing in life. When we have confidence in who we are, we are unstoppable. We can do anything and create anything! If we are pushing our own agendas on our children though, wanting them to play for this team or take this class because that is what we want them to do, we are then not allowing our children to follow their own heart and do what interests them. Their confidence is then stifled for they feel that they are not good enough since their desires are

DOI: 10.4324/9781003511847-7

not good enough for their parents or caregivers. What they truly want is not valued, and hence they are not valued. Let that sink in for a moment. How awful for our children to feel this way: that their interests are not important, hence, the way they think is not important.

With the crisis of mental health surrounding us, we need to look at how we can help rectify this epidemic, starting in our own students' homes.

We need to remind parents to allow their children to be who they are. Look them in the eye. Notice them. Have conversations with them and really listen. Put your own phone down and give them the gift of being consciously present for them and your time together. Notice, listen, and allow them to be the human being they are. We are all just human beings trying to navigate this life we have. We all have our own paths. Respect your child for being the individual they are and allow them to unfold and discover.

When children feel supported in their own homes, they are better able to make and keep healthy relationships. They know how to communicate better and articulate their wants and needs. Sit at the dinner table with your child. Have uninterrupted conversations. Make it a rule of no phones at the dinner table and cherish those 20 minutes of peace and connection before going separate ways in the world again. Ask questions, listen, and connect.

Help your child to feel their breath when they start to get wound from the challenges of life. Teach them to stop, and just feel their body breathe. Remind them of things they can do to calm themselves. Give them access to just being.

Diet

Eat from the earth. Fruits and vegetables offer all the nutrients we need to grow, think, and Be. If it comes from a plant, it is nourishment for our bodies and minds. If all we eat is crap, then we feel like crap. As adults we can totally relate to this as we have chowed down on our favorite processed food, only to then have to go lay on the couch because our stomach hurts from the excess sugar or processed chemicals. Our body feels that way because our digestive organs are trying to digest the unnatural substances that we have put in our body. It needs extra energy to digest, hence why we need to lie down to let our body get the junk food through our system. Kids are no different.

Being a mindful eater, consciously aware of what you are putting into your child's body and your own is a game changer. And yes, of course, there are times that call for special treats, but try not to make processed foods the norm.

Consciously being aware when you are eating is important too. Talk about the food you are eating. Where did you get it? Did you grow it? Prepare meals together.

Communicate by Listening

Have those difficult conversations with your children. They want to feel heard. They want to know that their ideas are valid, even if they are different from what you think. We need to just listen; refrain from talking and just hear our children out. You will end up learning something new about the person they are becoming and where their interests lie. Never deter them. Never put your own unfulfilled dreams on this human being who is different from you. Let them evolve. Let them grow into who they are meant to be. As they come to you with their hopes, dreams and fears become mindful of the interaction and truly listen. Love them unconditionally. Open your heart and you will find it full as you have this connection with your child. Validate their feelings. Tell them you love them.

And it is okay to ask your child questions during a serious conversation, and wait in the silence, for their answer. Sometimes children do not have the vocabulary to tell of their feelings or reasons. Respect that silence as they try to communicate verbally with you, using the words that they have. Once they give you their answers/reasons, you can then guide them with new vocabulary to name feelings or situations, but allow them to communicate with their own words first.

When you have these conversations with your child, validate them by telling them of a time when you felt the same way or had a similar experience. Let them know they are not alone. You were once like them too. Let them know your unconditional love.

Mindful Participation

Art classes, music classes, dance, theatre, essentially all the arts can all help a person become more mindful if it is their choice to participate. Spending time doing these activities brings their focus to whatever the task at hand is in front of them. They tap into creativity that they may not have known they had and again, help to build that self-confidence. Sports can obviously do the same if your child enjoys athletics. Being physical every day is important regardless if it is on a field, a hike, or through dance, as physical activity is good for our mental wellness and fostering mindfulness.

Gratitude

Having some sort of gratitude practice is key to a happy and flourishing life! Whether it is a discussion of things that happened during the day that filled your heart, a journaling exercise, conversation around the dinner table, a thankyou card, a picture; anything that shows one is grateful for the blessings in their life only opens our eyes to other blessings that surround us.

The simple mantra of "thank you" for whatever you are grateful for works, even if it is just for a cup of coffee, a quiet moment before walking into the grocery store, the smile of your child, an encounter with a stranger, a beautiful sky, the possibilities are endless! Find gratitude in your own daily life, no matter how small, and teach your children to do the same. Gratitude is life changing as our eyes will start to open to the abundance and beauty that surrounds us.

Wisdom from a Past Generation

My grandmother, Marge Seebode, and I had a lovely conversation on the beach, looking at the waves, feeling the ocean breeze, days before my oldest daughter's first day of kindergarten. Mema, as I called her, told me to expect that Noelani would have days of misbehavior ahead. She said that Noelani would most likely spend her days in the classroom, following all the rules, sitting in her seat, raising her hand, sharing with other students, being kind to other students even though some of those students would not be kind to her, all while learning new concepts and making friends. Mema told me that if Noelani was sassy at home, or sometimes not kind, to realize that she was trying out her independence and trying out her voice; that same voice that would get her in trouble potentially if she was to try it out in school.

Home is a safe space. A space for children to try out their voice. A place where they should feel comfortable to say that they just want to be quiet for some time and do their own thing. As adults, we understand how a day can be overwhelming, and how we want to unwind at the end of the day. Our children want this as well at times. When they become sassy, and try out their voice, use it as an opportunity to try humor in the home. Turn it into something funny so that a continued stronger relationship is established between you and your child. One of fun and humor; not of domination and control. Make it a funny moment but also a teachable one regarding respect for others and the opportunity to communicate calmly.

Making Mistakes

Making Mistakes is okay; it is how we learn. Mistakes get us to level up and to do something better the next time around. They are part of life and show us that we are evolving. Children should never be belittled for their mistakes, instead, they should be able to reflect without shame so that they see the opportunity to grow. And please don't ever use the word "shame" with your children.

Nobody has the right to inflict shame on any other being and doing so potentially sets up a lifetime of staying small and having low self-confidence due to the shame inflicted from a mistake. Use the opportunity instead to love your child, helping them understand that the world still rotates, the sun will still come up, and they can do things differently the next time around.

As a reminder for us parents who are perfectionists, Google has a 40% failure rate. That is certainly making mistakes, and Google wants to keep failing! Failing shows that you are trying, and trying better each time, by making something better. So, mistakes are good. It means we are creating, working, trying things out; it is all good, and part of evolving.

Albert Einstein said, "A person who never made a mistake never tried anything new."

Thomas Edison said, "I have not failed. I just found 10,000 ways that won't work." So let us encourage our children to try new things; to make those mistakes. Let's encourage them so they can have confidence in who they are and who they are evolving to be.

Self-control is a super power. Let us remember this for ourselves as parents and remind our children as well.

Support your child, in all of their endeavors, even if it is not your own. Let them know you support them. Just show up. Put the phone away and let them make eye contact with you. Let them know they are valued by you. Let them know they are loved.

Be aware of the relationships you are creating with your child. Are you unknowingly recreating that same trauma with your child that you went through? What words do you use with your child? Are you placing shame on them? Are you beating them down verbally? Are you trying to control who they are? Be consciously aware of how to speak to your child; how you interact with them. Be aware and just love. It is that simple. Just love them.

Go on field trips and have them live life fully. Go to an art gallery and notice. Take them on a hike and notice. Sit on the grass and stare at the clouds and notice. Do a five senses poem.

Have them say what they see, what they smell, what they taste, what they hear, and what they feel.

Just spend time with your child and listen to them. It is the greatest gift you can give them – your time.

Further Resources for Parents

♦ Books that support mindfulness in other arenas of life:
  Fire Child, Water Child by Stephen Scott Cowan, MD
  Super Me by Adi Benning
♦ *The Paper Girls Show Orgami Craft Book: 21 Folding Creations* by Global Tinker

The 30-Day Classroom Mindfulness Challenge

Are you ready to foster a classroom of peace? This challenge has precise things to do that take less than 10 minutes of your day to establish a peaceful, accepting, safe, nurturing, and joyful classroom. If you start this at the beginning of the year, you will establish mindfulness routines that will last the entire year, and really, into life. If you start at some other point in the year, you will still see the benefits.

Day 1: Watch Mini Meditation for Kids on YouTube.
Day 2: Have a positive affirmation on the board and ask students to journal what that affirmation means to them.
Day 3: Have students draw a picture of something or someone that makes them happy.
Day 4: Go outside and complete a mental five senses poem.
Day 5: Teach students how to breathe slowly using the breathing technique from the resource section.
Day 6: Watch a Mini Meditation for Kids on YouTube.
Day 7: Have students make a list of things they are grateful for.
Day 8: Have students write a thank you card.
Day 9: Take a walk outside and see what students can notice in nature.
Day 10: Listen to a Mini Meditations for Kids Podcast.

Day 11: Put on soothing music and have students just breathe and Be.

Day 12: Ask the students one of the journal questions from the resource section and have them write their response.

Day 13: Have students draw a picture or make a slide of things about themselves. Snippet of Me.

Day 14: Listen to the Podcast of Mini Meditations for Kids.

Day 15: How can I be a better friend? Journal.

Day 16: Have students find a quote that they connect to and journal about it.

Day 17: After some mindful breathing, share student quotes on the board anonymously.

Day 18: Have students try out a yoga pose and feel their breath while they are in the pose.

Day 19: Journal – What does peace mean to me?

Day 20: Watch a Mini Meditations for Kids on YouTube.

Day 21: Plant seeds in solo cups, having each student set an intention for their seed, and place them in the window to watch them grow.

Day 22: Journal – What would you like to grow in your life?

Day 23: Share student quotes again and have students connect to one and discuss why they like it.

Day 24: Have students listen to the Mini Meditations for Kids Podcast.

Day 25: Have students write a letter to a relative or friend.

Day 26: Watch a Mini Meditations for Kids YouTube Video.

Day 27: Draw a picture while listening to soft music.

Day 28: Blow bubbles.

Day 29: Listen to a Mini Meditations for Kids Podcast.

Day 30: Have students come up with their own positive affirmation.

If you start with the first six weeks, it will be an embedded routine for your class that you can continue with more quotes, discussions, mini meditations for kids, Just Be Time, drawing, whatever works for the culture of your classroom.

All resources can be found on Bringingmindfulnessintothec lassroom.com

When you have finished the 30 days of curriculum above, use the other resources within the book to continue, or other videos of mine as well as podcast recordings. Curtail what your classroom needs depending on the culture and/or dynamics and continue to have mindfulness as part of your classroom routine, even if it is just to Be.

B

Mindful Pages

Journal Prompts for Bringing Mindfulness into Your Own Life

Use the following journal prompts to learn more about yourself; hence to guide your own personal flourishing. Treat yourself to a new journal from a local bookstore, use these pages, or another format for you to write about yourself.

Use the following journal prompts to learn more about yourself; hence to guide your own personal flourishing. Treat yourself to a new journal from a local bookstore, use these pages, or another format for you to write about yourself.

Questions to Guide Personal Flourishing:
Write down three things that make you smile.

Write down a challenge that you enjoy.

Write down something you are proud of.

If you could do anything with your life, what would it be?

If you could live anywhere, where would it be and why?

If you could travel anywhere in the world, where would you go and why? What would you do? What would you hope to bring back with you? Who would you take?

What is your idea of a perfect weekend?

Who is one successful person you admire and why?

How would you serve others?

If you had $1000 to give to any non-profit charity, which one would you choose and why?

Write down three people who impacted your life?

What goal are you working on right now or would like to make?

What would you like people to know about you?

What is your wish for your life?

What can you do to make this world a better place?

What does Peace mean to me?

With the Questions to Guide Personal Flourishing in mind, where do you see opportunities to ask your students those same questions? You know your own routines of your classroom, it's culture and transitions. Can you find a handful of minutes here and there to connect with your students? Take a few minutes to jot down your thoughts.

How can I practice self-care?

List all the things that you are grateful for at this moment.

What is it that you want for your life?

Where should you place your energy today?

What fills your heart with joy?

What is your vision for your best life?

When you are your best version, what does that look like? What does it feel like?

About the Author

Tara Segree strives to promote the knowledge that inner peace is available to all individuals, regardless of backgrounds, perspectives, identity, religion, and/or ideology.

Tara's vision is to bring peace to the world through helping others recognize their strengths, thus giving them confidence to collaborate with others and create. She has witnessed the ripple effect of what meditation/mindfulness can do for humanity and strives for all people to access and step into a better version of themselves and continue to align with their highest potential.

Through education, workshops, and retreats, Tara helps others learn to be the architect of their own life by making conscious choices of peace and love each day. She helps people to tune in to their internal compass to live a life of purpose.

Living a life of peace, love, and light helps us to consciously make decisions that are for the greater good of humankind. Helping others to think in a way that is optimistic and positive raises the vibration of our world and establishes a blanket of peace worldwide.

No matter what is happening in our lives, peace, guidance, and clarity can be found by going within and being still and silent. We all have access to this peace, and when we tap into that peace daily, walking a life of peace becomes second nature. Things no longer trigger us. Challenges become avenues to create. We respond to life with peace, which only brings more joy and optimism into our life.

Walking a path of peace allows us to see the beauty that surrounds us every day. Walking a path of peace gives us clarity and decisiveness. Walking a path of peace gives us greater connection to the world around us. Beauty is found everywhere, if only we open our eyes and choose to see it.

Tara Segree has her Masters in Leadership in Teaching and is currently a Special Education English Teacher at Broadneck

High School in Annapolis, Maryland, as well as an adjunct faculty member at Notre Dame of Maryland University. She has been teaching students from age 2 to 81 for close to 20 years and believes that all people can be successful if we build upon one's own unique strengths and gifts, thus helping them find their passions and many purposes in life. Tara was the co-creator of the Student Alliance for Flourishing, recipient of the Innovative Educator of the Year accolade in 2021, and is a co-collaborator in Global Tinker's *Mini Meditations for Kids, The Paper Girls Show* Podcast, named by Common Sense Media as one of the Best Podcasts for Children in 2022 and 2023.

Tara was trained in mindfulness under the world renowned "mindbody health & wellness expert, mindful performance trainer, meditation teacher" and author davidji, and Suze Yalof Schwartz of Unplug Meditation in Los Angeles, California. She teaches students of all ages the positive personal and global impacts of living a life consciously, with purpose and peace.

Tara believes that the advancement of human consciousness is available to all and guides others on their personal journey by having them ask themselves the question: "What can I do to make this world a better place?" Tara helps others to be conscious creators of their own life by becoming architects of their life through the conscious choices that they make.

Combining wellness and education can only advance human progress and a more peaceful planet.

To bring professional developments for teachers, assemblies for students, and/or workshops for parents to your school, inquire at www.bringingmindfulnessintotheclassroom.com.

Acknowledgments

There are so many people in my life who have made me who I am today. All interactions, connections, and relationships have been the threads in the tapestry of my life. All of my challenges have helped me become the woman I am today. All of the beautiful people I have been blessed to interact with have helped me become the woman I am today. All of the brief interactions and connections with others have taught me lessons of love, hope, strength, and empowerment. I am forever grateful for everyone who has played a role in my life.

My strong and beautiful daughters Noelani, Malia, Allana, and Miele are the greatest gifts of my life. They have taught me how to live a life of integrity, openness, and authenticity, all while aligned with love. They gave me the courage to step into my truth and be the strong woman I was meant to be. They unknowingly forced me to take my power back to show how to be an independent woman, creating the life of beautiful abundance that is meant to be lived by all human beings, if only we are brave enough to do so. I will be forever grateful for those beautiful beings of mine for choosing me to be their mom, so that I would have the courage to live life fully, tethered forever to their hearts.

My fantastically phenomenal friends who have always supported me and my wild and crazy ideas. Thank you for being my biggest cheerleaders and applauding me from the first row, for without your wind, I would not have had the confidence to step into my truth. Your laughter, love, encouragement, and shenanigans have put such a zest into my life that I have had no choice but to embrace this beautiful world with optimism and joy. Your guidance through your insight has propelled my actions and steps as I navigate this world with peace, aligned with love. Some of you I have known for decades, and some not as long; regardless, your friendship is platinum, and one of the best parts of my life.

My dear dear fellow educators: boy it has been a ride. The comic relief of teaching this next generation along with all the challenges and heartbreaks that come along with our profession is worth it. May you always stay true to yourself and the love you have, to inspire and encourage students to think for themselves, to keep an open mind, and to lean in to hear others with different viewpoints; for we all come from different backgrounds, cultures, upbringing, experiences, etc., and that is what makes our world a beautiful place. May you continue to be brave and hold space for students to communicate their truth, and teach respect for all people. My collaborative teachers have been the best around. How blessed I have been in my profession to learn and work with each one of you.

The Human Flourishing Program at Harvard's Institute for Quantitative Social Science: Community of Practice named me Innovative Educator of the Year back in 2021 which opened my eyes to my capability and belief that what I was creating was respected and needed. This accolade truly helped me believe in myself even more.

Dr. Kristine Larson, who has believed in me from the first day we met, is still challenging me!

Sep Riahi and Olivia Levenson Korchagin from Global Tinker whose collaboration started a wave of peace to children around the world.

Last but not least, my mother Kathy Smith, who was not sure what to do with a child so strong willed, but eventually came to see the iridescent colors of my wings. Thank you Mom for your patience with me, your faith, and prayers that have spurred my journey. My sisters who have seen me grow in all stages, watering my soil with their nourishment when needed, and in turns, brothers, Lesa, Bonnie, extended family of cousins, aunts, nieces, nephews, outlaws, in-laws, all the threads of the big extended tapestry of my large and lively family. May we always choose peace, aligned with love.

And, of course, the support of the Divine Realm. All of my spiritual guides, angels, ancestors, who have been with me throughout my life; offering divine protection through all the lessons, and divine guidance and inspiration when I was ready to receive it.

Thank you to you, the reader, for it is through your own heart that "you can do your little part to bring peace to our world." *Bill Smith*

Blessings~

Printed in the United States
by Baker & Taylor Publisher Services